I0820923

INSIDE THE NFL

INDIANAPOLIS COLTS

by Charlie Beattie

An imprint of Abdo Publishing
abdobooks.com

ABDOBOOKS.COM

Published by Abdo Publishing, a division of ABDO, PO Box 398166, Minneapolis, Minnesota 55439.

Printed in China.
052025
092025

Cover Photos: Justin Edmonds/Getty Images Sport/Getty Images (Jonathan Taylor); George Gojkovich/Getty Images Sport/Getty Images (Peyton Manning)
Interior Photos: Justin Casterline/Getty Images Sport/Getty Images, 4–5, 6; Matt Patterson/AP Images, 7; Zach Bolinger/AP Images, 8, 9, 61 (bottom right); Abdo Publishing, 10–11, 58; William A. Smith/AP Images, 12–13; AP Images, 15, 19; Tony Tomsic/AP Images, 16; Focus on Sport/Getty Images, 17, 26, 28, 32, 34; Robert Riger/Hulton Archive/Getty Images, 18; Horace Cort/AP Images, 21; Harold Matosian/AP Images, 22; Robert Riger/Getty Images Sport/Getty Images, 23; Vernon Biever/AP Images, 24–25; Focus on Sport/Getty Images Sport/Getty Images, 27, 30, 36–37, 60 (bottom left); Kidwiler Collection/Diamond Images/Getty Images, 29; David Durochik/AP Images, 33; Al Messerschmidt Archive/AP Images, 35, 39, 45, 60 (bottom right), 63; Peter Read Miller/AP Images, 38; Bettmann/Getty Images, 40; Bill Kostroun/AP Images, 41; George Widman/AP Images, 42; Keith Srakocic/AP Images, 43, 61 (bottom left); Adam Nadel/AP Images, 44; Andy Lyons/Getty Images Sport/Getty Images, 46–47, 53, 57; Rusty Kennedy/AP Images, 48, 61 (top); Robert Laberge/Getty Images Sport/Getty Images, 49; Sandra Dukes/Getty Images Sport/Getty Images, 51; Chris Carlson/AP Images, 52; Darron Cummings/AP Images, 54; Greg Trott/AP Images, 55; Rob Carr/Getty Images Sport/Getty Images, 56; Kevin Sabitus/Getty Images Sport/Getty Images, 59

Editor: Chrös McDougall
Series Designer: Laura Graphenteen
Production Designer: Ryan Gale

Library of Congress Control Number: 2024948500

Publisher's Cataloging-in-Publication Data

Names: Beattie, Charlie, author.
Title: Indianapolis Colts / by Charlie Beattie
Description: Minneapolis, Minnesota: Abdo Publishing, 2026 | Series: Inside the NFL | Includes online resources and index.
Identifiers: ISBN 9781098296759 (lib. bdg.) | ISBN 9798384919278 (ebook)
Subjects: LCSH: Indianapolis Colts (Football team)--Juvenile literature. | National Football League--Juvenile literature. | Football teams--Juvenile literature. | American football--Juvenile literature.
Classification: DDC 796.333--dc23

CONTENTS

CHAPTER 1
TAYLOR MADE ... 4

CHAPTER 2
BALTIMORE BEGINNINGS ... 12

CHAPTER 3
SUPER COLTS ... 24

CHAPTER 4
INDIANAPOLIS BOUND ... 36

CHAPTER 5
REACHING THE TOP ... 46

TIMELINE ... 60
GLOSSARY ... 62
ONLINE RESOURCES ... 63
INDEX ... 64

Jonathan Taylor (28) breaks a tackle against the Jacksonville Jaguars in Week 17 of the 2020 season.

CHAPTER 1

TAYLOR MADE

JONATHAN TAYLOR TOOK A HANDOFF AND AIMED FOR THE RIGHT SIDE OF his offensive line. That avenue wasn't open. Dancing quickly to his left, the Indianapolis Colts running back burst through a tiny opening. As several Jacksonville Jaguars defenders tried to keep pace, Taylor exploded into the open field. He ran 56 yards before being pushed out of bounds at the Jaguars' 11-yard line. The first-quarter scamper was just a taste of what Taylor had in store for the day.

Indianapolis was hosting the Jaguars in Week 17 of the 2020 National Football League (NFL) season. Taylor's Colts entered with a record of 10–5. They stood one win shy of clinching a second playoff berth in three seasons. All they had to do was beat the lowly Jaguars. Jacksonville hadn't won since beating

Taylor rushed for more than 6,000 yards while scoring 50 touchdowns in three years at Wisconsin.

Indianapolis in the first week of the season. Now, on the last day of the season, Taylor set out to make sure they never came close to a second win.

ROOKIE SENSATION

The Colts had a long and proud history that included some all-time great offenses. But going into the 2020 NFL Draft, the team desperately needed offensive weapons. The season before,

Indianapolis had finished 25th out of 32 NFL teams in total offensive yardage. That lack of scoring had led to a disappointing 7-9 record.

Finding elite players in the draft is always a challenge. The job was made even harder for Indianapolis because it didn't have a first-round pick. The Colts had traded it to the San Francisco 49ers for defensive end DeForest Buckner. Instead, the Colts got aggressive in the second round. After picking wide receiver Michael Pittman Jr. 34th overall, Indianapolis made another trade to grab the 41st pick. With it, the Colts selected Taylor.

It seemed like a steal. The former Wisconsin Badger had run for more than 2,000 yards twice in his college career. He left the school after just three seasons, two of them as an All-American.

The Colts already had a starting running back in Marlon Mack. Colts coach Frank Reich originally planned to ease Taylor into the NFL, allowing him to learn behind Mack. But when Mack suffered a season-ending injury in Week 1, Taylor stepped in. After some early ups and downs, the 5-foot, 10-inch, 226-pound back rushed

Coach Frank Reich, *right*, had a record of 40-33-1 in five years with the Colts.

for 398 yards and five touchdowns over four games in December. That earned him the league's Offensive Rookie of the Month Award. The Jaguars arrived in Indianapolis soon after for a Week 17 matchup.

Taylor's 253-yard performance against the Jaguars was his third 100-yard game of the 2020 season.

HISTORIC DAY

Taylor's 56-yard run set up an early Colts touchdown. On the team's next drive, Taylor had a two-yard touchdown run wiped out by a face mask penalty. Indianapolis had to settle for a field goal to make it 10–0. In the second quarter, Taylor finally hit pay dirt. Three plays after a Jacksonville fumble, the star rookie plunged in from one yard out for his 10th rushing touchdown of the season. It helped the Colts build a 20–0 lead. Indianapolis's route to the postseason looked clear.

Finishing the job wouldn't be so easy, though. A pair of Jacksonville touchdown passes cut the Colts' lead to 20–14 with 6:26 left in the third quarter. That score stood deep into the fourth quarter, too. But when the Colts got the ball back at the 50-yard line with 4:26 to play, everyone knew who was getting the ball.

All game, Taylor had been piling up rushing yards. He jogged back onto the field with 191, just 28 shy of the Colts' single-game record, set in 2004 by Edgerrin James. And on first down, Taylor picked up five more.

AN UNSEEN RECORD

Jonathan Taylor's record day against the Jaguars took place in a mostly empty stadium. Because of the COVID-19 pandemic, the NFL did not allow full stadiums during the 2020 season. As Taylor marched over the Jaguars in Week 17, only 9,976 fans were able to watch in person at Lucas Oil Stadium in Indianapolis. In normal times, the stadium seats more than 60,000 fans.

On second down, the Jaguars set up with eight players near the line of scrimmage to stop the run. Indianapolis quarterback Philip Rivers took the snap out of the shotgun formation. Taylor stood to the quarterback's left and took the handoff. As Taylor advanced toward the line, a Jacksonville defender blocked his path. With a quick shake of his shoulders, Taylor sent the defender stumbling. The Colts running back eased past and sprinted untouched to the end zone. The 45-yard run sealed a playoff spot and put Taylor in the record books. It wouldn't be the last time Taylor made his mark in an Indianapolis uniform.

Taylor breaks away for his 45-yard score late in the game against the Jaguars.

NFL TEAMS MAP

NFC EAST

NFC WEST

NFC NORTH

NFC SOUTH

AFC

AFC EAST
- BUFFALO BILLS
- MIAMI DOLPHINS
- NEW ENGLAND PATRIOTS
- NEW YORK JETS

AFC WEST
- DENVER BRONCOS
- KANSAS CITY CHIEFS
- LAS VEGAS RAIDERS
- LOS ANGELES CHARGERS

AFC NORTH
- BALTIMORE RAVENS
- CINCINNATI BENGALS
- CLEVELAND BROWNS
- PITTSBURGH STEELERS

AFC SOUTH
- HOUSTON TEXANS
- INDIANAPOLIS COLTS
- JACKSONVILLE JAGUARS
- TENNESSEE TITANS

Carroll Rosenbloom, *second from left*, brought football back to Baltimore in 1953.

CHAPTER 2

BALTIMORE BEGINNINGS

THE NFL WAS FOUNDED IN 1920, AND BY THE 1940S IT WAS AN established league. Other cities wanted to get in on professional football. However, the NFL wasn't interested in adding a lot of new teams. So, in 1946, a new league emerged to give more cities an opportunity. The All-America Football Conference (AAFC) began with eight teams. One of them was the Miami Seahawks. But after one disastrous season during which the head coach quit halfway through, the Seahawks moved to Baltimore. There, they were renamed the Colts in honor of Maryland's long history of horse breeding and racing.

The AAFC folded in 1949. Three of its teams joined the NFL. The Colts were one of them, but their stay in the league was short. Baltimore's franchise shut down after the 1950 season.

THE TRIANGLES

The Dallas Texans franchise whose players migrated to Baltimore actually started in Ohio as the Dayton Triangles in 1916. The Triangles played in the NFL through 1929. Then they moved to Brooklyn and became the Dodgers. Over the next 23 years, the team would be known as the Dodgers, Brooklyn Tigers, Boston Yanks, New York Bulldogs, New York Yanks, and finally the Texans. Some fans consider the modern Colts descendants of the Triangles, though that is not officially recognized by the NFL.

The NFL returned to Baltimore just three years later. Investor Carroll Rosenbloom started a new team, which he also called the Colts. That was ultimately the only connection between the two franchises, though.

The new Colts struggled early. Most of their players had come from the Dallas Texans, a team that folded after the 1952 season. Without a lot of talent, the Colts played to a 3-9 record in 1953. But help was on the way.

JOHNNY U

Before the 1954 season, the Colts hired Weeb Ewbank as the team's new head coach. The former naval officer slowly put together a winning team. Ewbank inherited talented defensive lineman Gino Marchetti from the Texans roster. In 1954, he added future Hall of Fame receiver Raymond Berry through the NFL Draft. Over the following seasons, Ewbank drafted other stars such as tackle Jim Parker, center Dick Szymanski, halfback Lenny Moore, and fullback Alan Ameche. However, it was a player Ewbank picked up off the scrap heap to be a backup who truly transformed the Colts.

In 1955, the Pittsburgh Steelers drafted quarterback Johnny Unitas out of Louisville. The Steelers barely gave him a chance and cut him before the season started. Unitas began working

Jim Parker was Baltimore's top pick in the 1957 draft. He reached eight Pro Bowls in 11 years with the Colts.

construction while playing semiprofessional football on the weekends. The Colts signed him in 1956 to back up starter George Shaw. Unitas's first professional pass was intercepted and returned for a touchdown. It was a bad beginning to what would become a legendary career.

In the fourth game of the season, Shaw suffered a broken leg. Unitas entered the game against the Chicago Bears and immediately took over as the team's star. He finished the season with 1,498 passing yards and nine touchdowns. That put him among the league's other great quarterbacks.

The Colts signed Johnny Unitas for $7,000 in 1956.

Considered by many to be the first modern quarterback, Unitas had a rocket arm and ran an offense filled with fake handoffs and complicated plays. Most of the time, Unitas called those plays himself in the huddle rather than receiving them from a coach on the sideline. But Unitas's greatest attribute might have been his toughness. One opponent remembered that "Johnny U" seemed to like taking hits during games. He couldn't be intimidated. By the 1957 season, Unitas was Baltimore's unquestioned starter.

Raymond Berry caught 12 passes for 178 yards and a touchdown in the 1958 NFL Championship Game.

He led the NFL with 24 touchdown passes, most of which went to Moore, Berry, or wideout Jim Mutscheller.

THE GREATEST GAME

Despite missing two games in 1958, Unitas led the NFL in touchdown passes while helping the Colts to a 9–3 record. He was still nursing three broken ribs when the Colts reached the NFL Championship Game against the New York Giants on December 28, 1958. At the time, football was rapidly gaining popularity, but baseball remained America's favorite sport. However, as TV became more popular in the 1950s, networks realized that football worked perfectly for the new medium. Compared to other sports, football was easy for fans at home to follow on TV.

Roughly 50 million people tuned in to watch the 1958 title game on NBC. Another 64,000 were in the stands at New York's

Yankee Stadium. What they saw changed football forever. Between the two teams, there were a dozen future Hall of Famers on the field. Though the game was sloppy early with several turnovers, the Colts managed to build a 14–3 lead on a touchdown run by Ameche and a 15-yard scoring pass from Unitas to Berry.

Unitas looks to pass during the 1958 NFL title game.

The Giants clawed their way back. They took a 17–14 lead early in the fourth quarter. That remained the score when Unitas and the Colts' offense took over at the Baltimore 14 with two minutes to play. Unitas and Berry connected three times on the drive. The Colts maneuvered to New York's 13-yard line with seven seconds left. Baltimore kicker Steve Myhra finished it off with a 20-yard field goal to tie the game. Unitas's drive became known as the "two-minute drill," a term that is still used today to describe late drives when a team is trailing.

The tie score then created confusion. The NFL had adopted a sudden-death overtime period for playoff games in 1946. But in the 12 years since, the extra period had never been used. Unitas later said that he and his teammates didn't know what overtime was until the referee called the captains out for a coin toss.

The Giants won the toss but quickly went three-and-out and punted. Unitas then engineered another long drive. In 12 plays, the Colts drove 79 yards to the Giants' 1. On third-and-goal, Unitas handed the ball to Ameche, who plowed through a huge hole and into the end zone to win the game. Before the fullback could get up off the ground, fans had rushed out of the stands to join the celebration.

GOING DARK

The millions watching the 1958 NFL Championship Game at home nearly missed the dramatic finish. As the Colts neared the end zone on their final drive, a mishap on the TV broadcast knocked the game off the air. Producers briefly got the officials to stop the game so the picture could be restored. By the time Alan Ameche scored the winning touchdown, the game was back on TV.

Alan Ameche, *center*, powers through a hole to win the 1958 NFL title game in overtime.

The thrilling contest quickly became known as the "Greatest Game Ever Played." It supercharged the growth of the NFL. Soon, TV networks were scrambling to air as many games as they could. By the early 1960s, football was rocketing past baseball in popularity. And in Unitas, the Colts had the sport's biggest star. His clean-cut looks and incredible play made him the idol of football fans all over the country.

BACK-TO-BACK

Unitas followed up his 1958 heroics by winning the NFL's Most Valuable Player (MVP) Award in 1959. He also became the first quarterback ever to top 30 touchdown passes in an NFL season, finishing with 32. And with a 9–3 record, the Colts once again faced the Giants in the championship.

This time Baltimore's Memorial Stadium hosted the game. The Colts started well, taking a 7–0 lead in the first quarter on a 60-yard pass from Unitas to Moore. However, Baltimore's offense then stalled. By the end of the third, the Giants had taken a 9–7 lead.

The Colts' offense woke up in the fourth quarter in a big way. Unitas rushed for a 4-yard touchdown to retake the lead. He then threw a 12-yard touchdown pass to rookie receiver Jerry Richardson to make it 21–9. Finally, defensive back Johnny Sample clinched the victory by intercepting New York quarterback Charlie Conerly and sprinting 42 yards for a touchdown.

The Colts had the look of a dynasty. And though the team was loaded with talent, many placed the success on the right arm of Unitas. Legendary coach Vince Lombardi, who had been New York's

Lenny Moore had more than 5,000 rushing yards and 6,000 receiving yards in his 12-year NFL career.

defensive coordinator in the 1958 title game, said of Unitas, "Without him they're just ordinary. With him, they're great. He's the greatest quarterback I've ever seen."

> ***"WITHOUT HIM THEY'RE JUST ORDINARY. WITH HIM, THEY'RE GREAT. HE'S THE GREATEST QUARTERBACK I'VE EVER SEEN."***
>
> ***—VINCE LOMBARDI ON JOHNNY UNITAS***

Even with Unitas, the Colts couldn't keep up their championship ways. Throughout the early 1960s, some of Baltimore's other stars suffered injuries, and the team limped through three seasons in the middle of the NFL's West Division. After a 7–7 season in 1962, Rosenbloom made a big decision. He fired Ewbank despite nine mostly successful seasons and two championships.

In Ewbank's place, Rosenbloom hired Don Shula, who had played for the Colts as a defensive back from 1953 to 1956. At 33 years old, he became the youngest head coach in NFL history at the time. And by his second season, in 1964, he had the Colts back to their winning ways. Baltimore finished 12–2 as stars such as Moore and

Don Shula is carried off the field after the Colts clinched a spot in the 1964 NFL title game.

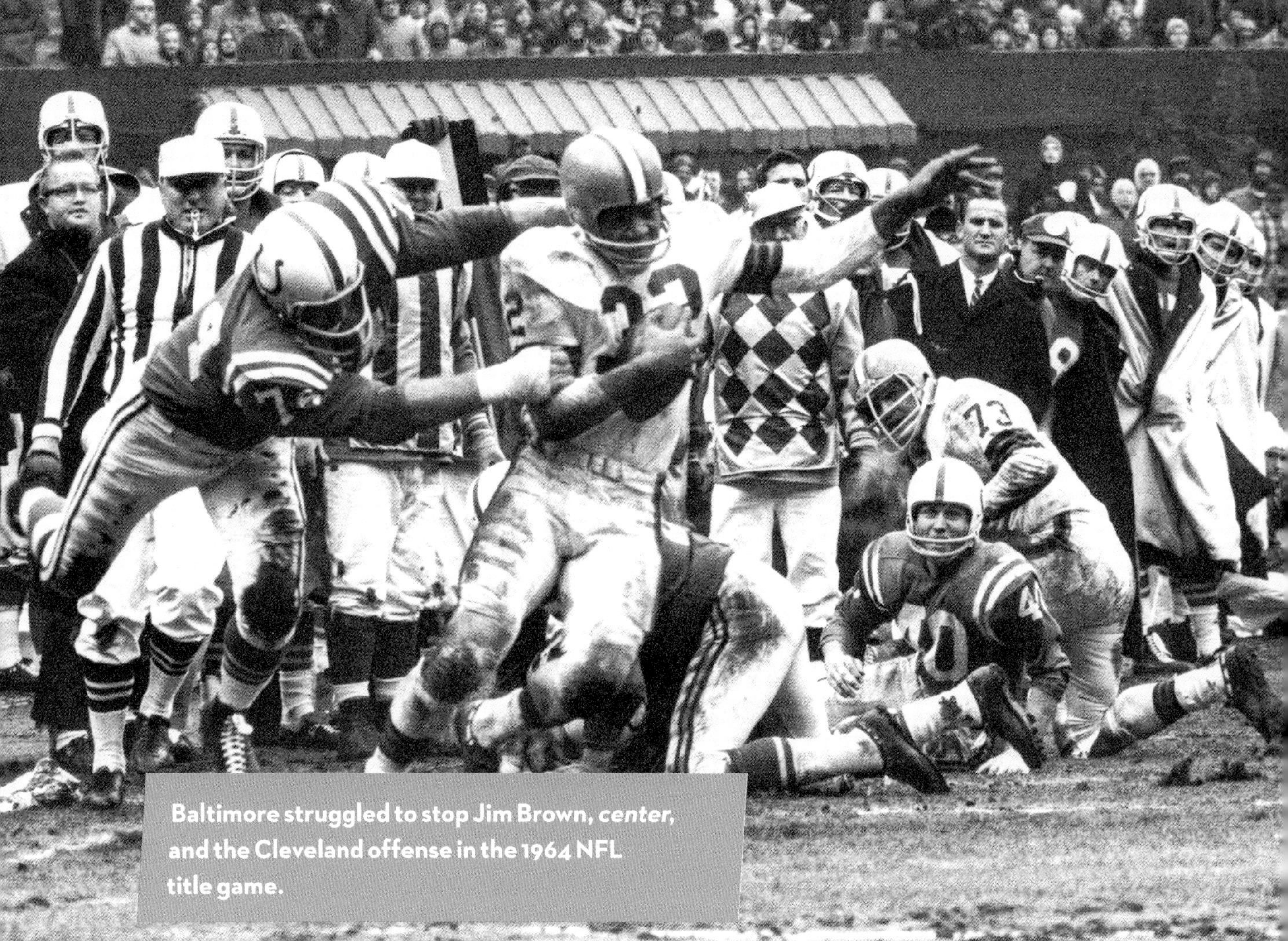

Baltimore struggled to stop Jim Brown, *center*, and the Cleveland offense in the 1964 NFL title game.

Berry were healthy again. Unitas also had a new receiving threat in second-year tight end John Mackey.

In the NFL Championship Game, Baltimore faced the Cleveland Browns. Experts expected the Colts to win, but Unitas delivered a flat performance. He threw for only 95 yards, and the Browns intercepted him twice. The all-time great was upstaged by Cleveland quarterback Frank Ryan. The veteran quarterback threw three touchdown passes, all to receiver Gary Collins, as the Browns routed Baltimore 27–0. The blowout loss was a disappointing end to a great season, but it was also the start of a new and successful era under Shula.

Tom Matte ran for 4,646 yards as a member of the Colts between 1961 and 1972.

CHAPTER 3

SUPER COLTS

WITH A 10–3–1 RECORD, THE 1965 COLTS FINISHED EVEN WITH the Green Bay Packers at the top of the NFL's West Division. That meant a one-game playoff was needed to decide who would face the Cleveland Browns for the league championship. Colts coach Don Shula had a big problem, though. His team had no quarterbacks. With both Johnny Unitas and backup Gary Cuozzo injured, Shula was forced to start running back Tom Matte under center.

Despite that, the Colts built a 10–0 halftime lead thanks to a fumble-recovery touchdown by linebacker Don Shinnick. But the Packers, the NFL's dynasty team of the 1960s, fought back in the second half. Late in the fourth quarter, the Packers lined up for a 22-yard field-goal attempt. Though many thought Don Chandler's kick missed wide, the officials called it good to tie the score 10–10. After Baltimore kicker Lou Michaels missed a potential game-winning kick in overtime, Chandler drilled a 25-yard field goal, and the Packers moved on.

A SUPER UPSET

As the Colts and Packers were battling for the 1965 league title, the NFL was changing. The American Football League (AFL) had started play in 1960. At first, few thought the AFL would be able to challenge the NFL. By the middle of the decade, the upstart league had done just that. Rather than compete against each other, the leagues decided to merge. In 1970, the AFL's teams would officially become part of the NFL.

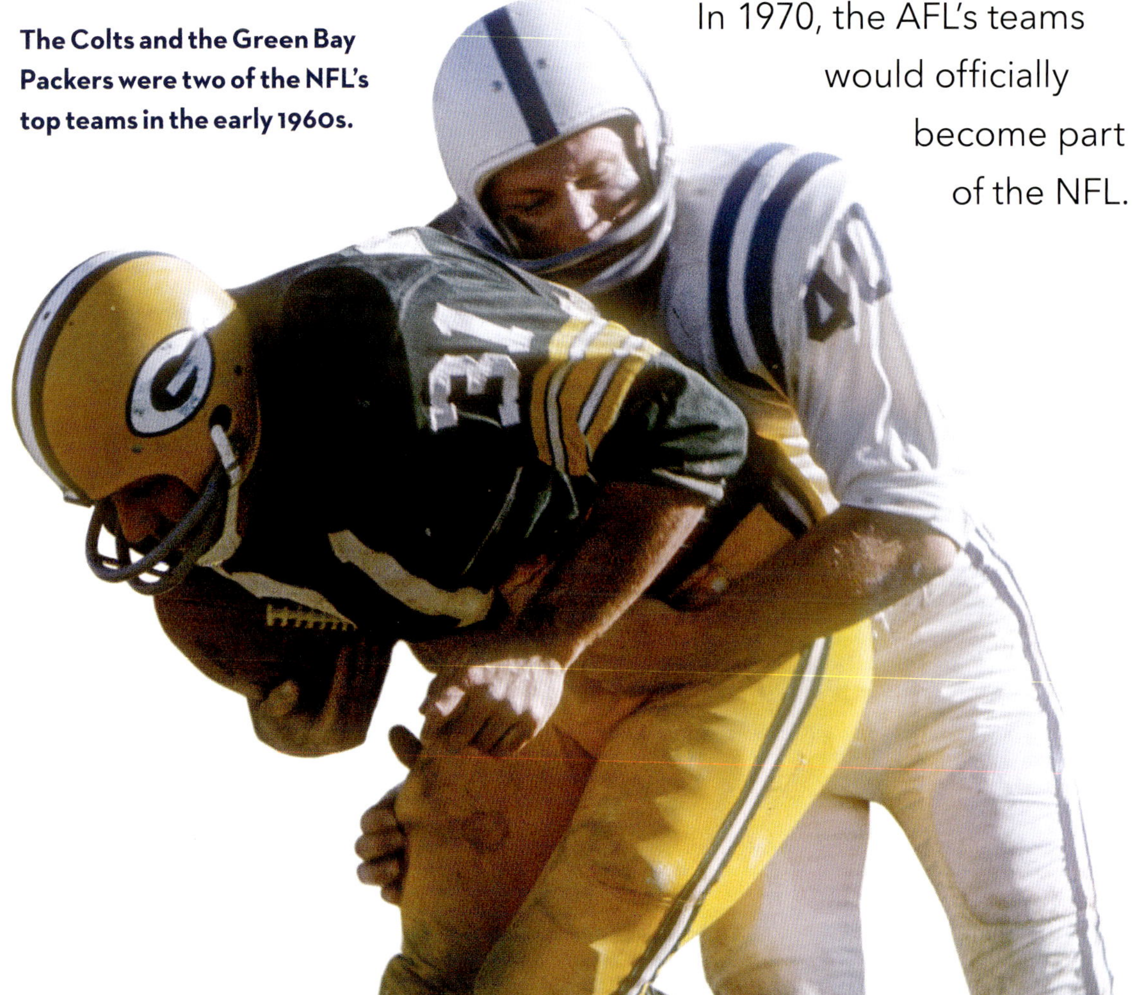

The Colts and the Green Bay Packers were two of the NFL's top teams in the early 1960s.

Johnny Unitas had a streak of 47 straight games with a touchdown pass in the 1960s, a record that stood until 2012.

Until then, the leagues decided their champions should meet in a postseason title game starting in 1966. This game would soon be known as the Super Bowl. The Colts could only watch as the dominant Packers easily won each of the first two Super Bowls. But in 1968, the Packers faded, and the Colts were once again on the rise.

Unitas remained a threat at quarterback. That showed in 1967, when he earned MVP honors after leading the Colts to an 11-1-2 record. But at 35 years old, he was starting to show the wear and tear of years of hits. And when he injured his elbow before the 1968 season began, Baltimore fans were worried.

In stepped Earl Morrall. Shula traded for the veteran quarterback after Unitas's injury. Morrall responded by throwing a league-high 26 touchdown passes and winning the NFL MVP Award. Even when Unitas was healthy again, Morrall kept the starting job. He led the Colts to a 13–1 record, and then they opened the playoffs by beating the Minnesota Vikings. Next they demolished the Browns 34–0 in the NFL Championship Game.

Earl Morrall, *left*, scrambles during a game against the Los Angeles Rams in 1968.

Baltimore linebacker Dennis Gaubatz (53) looks on as Joe Namath (12) drops back for the New York Jets in Super Bowl III.

That set up a matchup with the AFL's New York Jets in Super Bowl III. Most thought the Colts would win easily. The team had a great coach, several future Hall of Fame players, and the league's previous two MVPs at quarterback. But the Jets had a pair of secret weapons. The first was Weeb Ewbank, the former Baltimore coach who was now leading the Jets. The second was a confident young quarterback named Joe Namath.

A few days before the game, Namath got tired of hearing about how the Colts were going to roll over his Jets. At a banquet, he told a crowd of people that he was sure the Jets would win. Not many people took him seriously. Ewbank and some other Jets were upset that he had even made the statement. But when the game started, things started to unravel for Baltimore. Morrall completed only six passes and threw three interceptions. Unitas came in and didn't fare much better. He completed only 11 of his 24 attempts and threw a pick of his own. Along the way, Matte lost a fumble as well.

The Colts gained more than 300 yards in Super Bowl III but turned the ball over five times.

All the turnovers helped the Jets win 16–7. The game is remembered as one of the greatest upsets in sports history. Many consider the 1968 Colts to be one of the best teams to not win a title. Meanwhile, the game helped the Super Bowl become a cultural phenomenon.

THE BLUNDER BOWL

Shula quickly built a reputation as one of the best coaches in the NFL. In his first six seasons, the Colts won 63 regular-season games. Shula was named the NFL's Coach of the Year three times. But after Baltimore missed the playoffs in 1969, Shula surprised many by leaving for Miami, where the Dolphins offered him a chance to coach and own part of the team.

The situation frustrated Colts owner Carroll Rosenbloom, and the NFL later punished the Dolphins for how they went about the hire. But ultimately Baltimore needed a new head coach. Rosenbloom decided to promote assistant coach Don McCafferty. Whereas Shula had been a demanding head coach, McCafferty was much more easygoing. His laid-back personality helped the veteran Colts get back on top in 1970.

A new coach wasn't the only change that year. The AFL and NFL had officially merged. The former NFL became the National Football Conference (NFC), while the AFL was renamed the American Football Conference (AFC). Since the NFL had more teams, a few of the league's franchises switched to the AFC to balance things out. The Colts were one of them, along with the Browns and the Pittsburgh Steelers.

Baltimore finished 11–2–1, besting Shula's 10–4 Dolphins in the AFC East. Unitas, back as the team's starting quarterback, looked like his old self in playoff wins over the Cincinnati Bengals and Oakland Raiders. In those two games, the 37-year-old quarterback threw for a combined 390 yards and three touchdowns without an interception. After beating the Raiders 27–17 in the AFC title game, the Colts squared off with the Dallas Cowboys in Super Bowl V on January 17, 1971.

Neither team played well. The Cowboys committed four turnovers and 10 penalties. Unitas and Morrall both played, and the Colts quarterback duo threw three interceptions. The Colts also lost four fumbles. With 11 turnovers, Super Bowl V became known as the "Blunder Bowl."

Don McCafferty chats with Earl Morrall on the sidelines during Super Bowl V in January 1971.

> **"I WAS ACTUALLY EMBARRASSED TO COME BACK OUT OF THE LOCKER ROOM (AFTER HALFTIME)."**
>
> **—BOB VOGEL**

"I was actually embarrassed to come back out of the locker room (after halftime)," Colts offensive tackle Bob Vogel said.

However, between the mistakes, the Colts made two memorable plays. The first came in the second quarter with the team trailing 6–0. From his own 25, Unitas dropped back and fired a pass that was tipped twice. Somehow, the ball ended up in the hands of tight end John Mackey, who raced to the end zone. However, the Cowboys blocked kicker Jim O'Brien's extra-point attempt, and the score remained tied.

The score was 13–13 in the final minute when the Colts intercepted Dallas quarterback Craig Morton for a third time. Baltimore took over inside the Cowboys' 30. After running a few plays to kill the clock, O'Brien trotted out with nine seconds left. Without buttoning up his helmet chin strap, he booted the game-winning field goal.

It wasn't a pretty win. Fifty years after the game, the Colts' seven turnovers remained a record for a winning team. Baltimore led the game for only the final five seconds. Meanwhile, Dallas linebacker Chuck Howley is still the only player from a losing team to win Super Bowl MVP. However, for a Colts team that had been embarrassed in a Super Bowl upset two years earlier, no one cared about style points. The Colts were champions.

JOHN MACKEY

Before John Mackey joined the NFL, few tight ends caught passes. But Mackey's breakaway ability changed the position. In the 1966 season alone, he caught six touchdown passes of at least 50 yards. After his career ended, Mackey became the head of the players' union, and in that role his main goal was to fight for better health care for retired players.

THE TRADE

Tired of battling with the city for a new stadium, Rosenbloom had long wanted to get out of Baltimore. He found his opportunity in 1972, when the Los Angeles Rams went up for sale.

However, Rosenbloom couldn't buy the Los Angeles franchise without selling the Colts first. Selling his team in Baltimore would cost Rosenbloom a fortune in taxes, so he got creative.

Rosenbloom organized a deal in which Chicago businessman Robert Irsay would buy the Rams. The two would then trade franchises. Irsay would become the Colts' owner, and Rosenbloom would move to Los Angeles and take over the Rams. When the NFL didn't object, one of the strangest trades in American sports history took place. However, even in the hands of a new owner, the battle over the Colts' future in Baltimore was only just beginning.

John Mackey was enshrined in the Pro Football Hall of Fame in 1992.

Robert Irsay owned the Colts from 1972 until his death in 1997.

Ted Marchibroda won 71 games over two stints as head coach of the Colts.

CHAPTER 4

INDIANAPOLIS BOUND

At his best, Johnny Unitas was a game-changing superstar for the Colts. By 1972, however, the legendary quarterback was 39 years old and no longer at the top of his game. That year marked his fifth in a row throwing more interceptions than touchdowns. Baltimore also posted its first losing record in 16 seasons. So, as the team embarked on a new era in ownership, it began a new era at quarterback too. Prior to the 1973 season, the Colts traded Unitas to the San Diego Chargers.

The Colts moved on, but the team didn't return to its winning ways until 1975. Before that season, Baltimore hired Ted Marchibroda as its new head coach. He turned a team that had been 2–12 the year before into a 10–4 division winner. However, the Colts lost their first playoff game to the Pittsburgh Steelers.

A year later, Baltimore's offense became the best in football. Led by MVP quarterback Bert Jones and versatile running back Lydell Mitchell, the Colts averaged nearly 30 points per game. The defense, nicknamed the "Sack Pack," helped the Colts to another division title. However, once again they were routed by the Steelers in the playoffs, losing 40–14. The following year was a similar story. The Colts won the East Division but lost in overtime to the Oakland Raiders.

Bert Jones (7) led the NFL with 3,104 passing yards in 1976 and threw 24 touchdowns.

THE MIDNIGHT MOVE

Marchibroda was a well-liked coach, but he had to deal with constant interference from Robert Irsay. The opinionated owner would sometimes show up in the locker room during halftime. There, he might scream at everyone or even tell the coach to bench certain players. A previous coach had been fired during a game for refusing to take out his starting quarterback. At one point, Marchibroda briefly quit so he didn't have to put up with Irsay's antics anymore.

When Irsay wasn't in the locker room, he was fighting his players for every dollar. His penny-pinching ways cost the team stars such as Mitchell and defensive end John Dutton. Irsay traded them both in the late 1970s to avoid paying them bigger contracts.

However, Irsay's biggest fight was with the city of Baltimore. The Colts played in Memorial Stadium, which had been built in 1922. Carroll Rosenbloom had wanted it replaced when he was the owner, and Irsay wanted the same. However, the city was not willing to help pay for a new building.

After years of political disputes, the battle came to a bizarre end in late March 1984. Irsay had been considering an offer from the city of Indianapolis to move the team there. The Colts could play in the state's brand-new Hoosier Dome. The Baltimore government

The Hoosier Dome was a key component in the Colts' move to Indianapolis.

responded by attempting to claim eminent domain over the team. Under that law, the city could pay Irsay and take over the team, then keep it in Baltimore.

Before the law could take effect, Irsay acted. In the middle of the night of March 28, a fleet of moving trucks showed up at the team's facilities. By morning, every piece of the Baltimore Colts franchise was on the move to Indiana.

The city of Baltimore was stunned. Just two months earlier, Irsay had said he wasn't moving the team. Among those angry with Irsay were many former Colts players. Unitas led the charge by condemning the move. He severed all ties with the Colts.

ELWAY OPTS OUT

The Colts held the top pick in the 1983 NFL Draft. Everyone knew the top prize was Stanford quarterback John Elway. But Elway wanted nothing to do with the chaos in Baltimore. He told the Colts that if the team drafted him, he would play professional baseball instead. The Colts did draft Elway, but one week later they traded him to the Denver Broncos. There, Elway won two Super Bowls on his way to the Hall of Fame.

CARDIAC COLTS

Indianapolis was happy to have a team, even if the squad that moved to the city wasn't very good. The Colts had not had a winning season since 1977. In 1981, the Colts allowed an NFL-record 533 points while finishing 2–14.

It took a few years for things to get better, but in 1987 the Colts surprised the league by finishing 9–6 and

Eric Dickerson (29) set a Colts record with his 1,659 rushing yards in 1988. The mark stood until 2000.

winning the AFC East in a strike-shortened season. In the middle of the season, the Colts made a bold trade for star running back Eric Dickerson. The 6-foot, 3-inch, 220-pound back rushed for more than 1,000 yards in just nine games. The next year he led the league with 1,659 rushing yards, but the Colts missed the playoffs.

In 1992, Irsay convinced Marchibroda to come back as coach. By 1995, he had the scrappy team back in the playoffs. The Colts were an exciting team that always seemed to play in close games, which earned them the nickname "Cardiac Colts."

Leading the way was quarterback Jim Harbaugh, who had a knack for coming from behind in games. Harbaugh quickly became known as "Captain Comeback." But the veteran signal-caller didn't do it alone. A year earlier, the Colts had drafted running back Marshall Faulk from San Diego State. Faulk could do it all.

The shifty runner racked up more than 1,000 rushing yards while also leading the team in receptions.

Jim Harbaugh had three fourth-quarter comebacks and four game-winning drives during the 1995 season.

After posting a 9-7 record, the Colts reached the playoffs for just the second time since moving to Indianapolis. However, Faulk left the wild-card game against the San Diego Chargers after being injured on the first play. In his place, backup Zach Crockett rushed for 147 yards. That included a clinching 66-yard touchdown run in the fourth quarter as the Colts won 35–20.

The next week, the Colts survived a trip to frozen Kansas City. With the Chiefs trailing 10–7, their kicker Lin Elliott missed a potential tying field-goal attempt in the final minute. Now one win from the Super Bowl, the Colts went to Pittsburgh to take on the Steelers. In another tight game, Indianapolis trailed 20–16 with 1:34 left. As he had all season, Harbaugh led the team down the field. The Colts reached the Pittsburgh 29 with time for one more play. Harbaugh launched a Hail Mary pass into the end zone.

Aaron Bailey (80) fails to catch a late Hail Mary in the 1995 AFC Championship Game that would have sent the "Cardiac Colts" to the Super Bowl.

Several players went up for it. Colts receiver Aaron Bailey, while falling onto his back, tried to grab the ball on the way down. Instead, the ball bounced off his chest and hit the ground. The Colts fell one game short of the Super Bowl.

A GREAT DECISION

The Colts' breakout 1995 season didn't lead to sustained success. Marchibroda left the team to become coach of the new Baltimore Ravens in 1996. And though the Colts made the playoffs under new coach Lindy Infante, they fell in the wild-card round. A year later, the team collapsed to a 3-13 record. That same year, Irsay died, and his son, Jim, took over as the team owner.

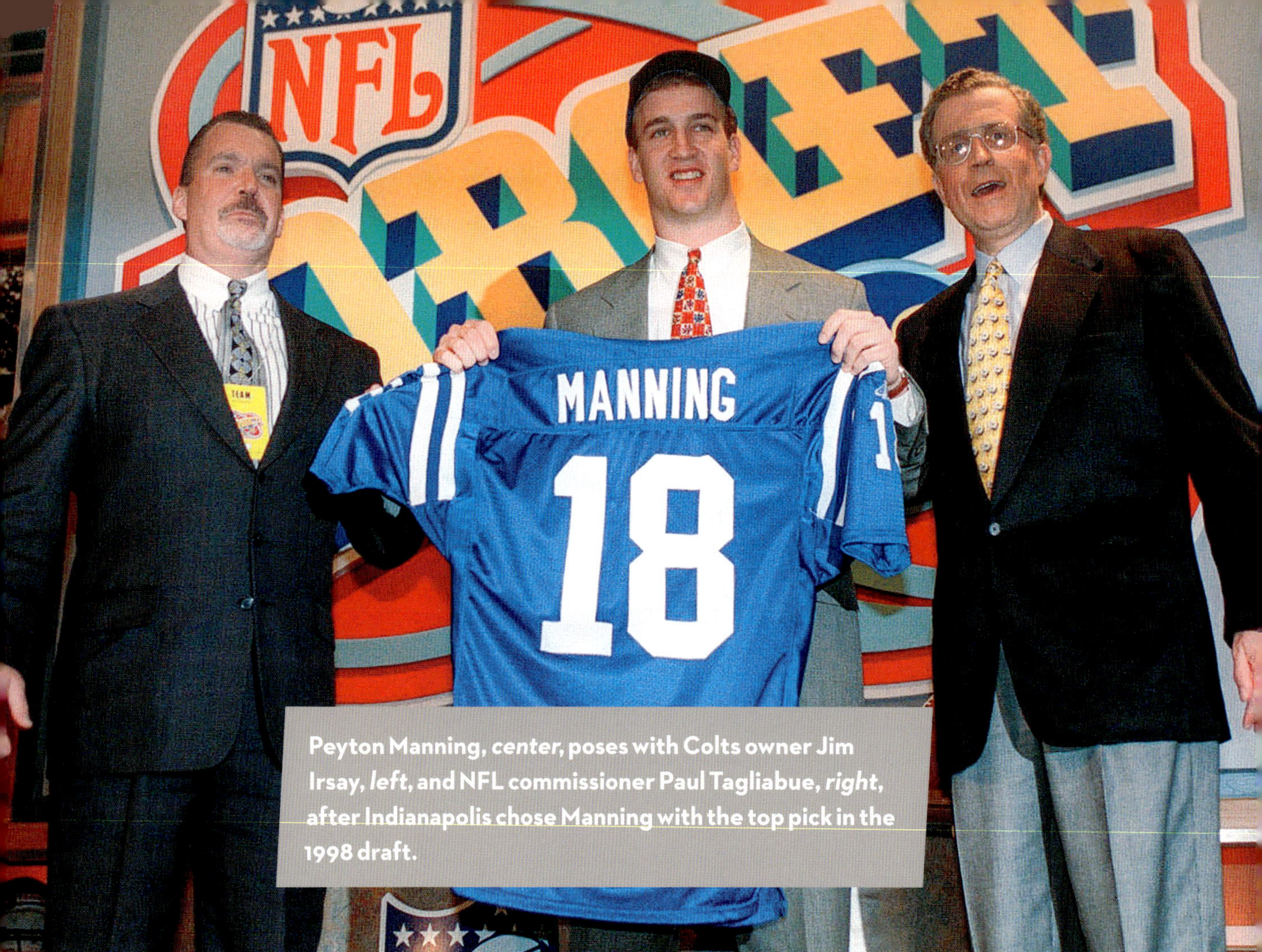

Peyton Manning, *center*, poses with Colts owner Jim Irsay, *left*, and NFL commissioner Paul Tagliabue, *right*, after Indianapolis chose Manning with the top pick in the 1998 draft.

Jim Irsay and Colts general manager Bill Polian soon had a huge decision to make. The Colts held the top pick, giving them a choice between two highly touted quarterbacks. Peyton Manning of Tennessee was the son of former NFL quarterback Archie Manning. The younger Manning was thought of as a football genius. On the other hand, Washington State's Ryan Leaf had a cannon of an arm.

In the end, the Colts went with Manning. It turned out to be one of the best decisions in football history. Leaf struggled with the San Diego Chargers and was out of the NFL within four years. Meanwhile, Manning became the Colts' best quarterback since Johnny Unitas.

It didn't happen right away, though. Working with new coach Jim Mora, Manning led the NFL with 28 interceptions as a rookie, while the Colts finished 3–13. But Manning also set rookie records with 3,739 passing yards and 26 touchdowns. Working with veteran offensive coordinator Tom Moore, Manning eventually became the league's most feared passer. On each play, he would scan the defense before the snap, identify the weak spots, and adjust the play based on what he saw. Few teams had an answer.

It helped that Indianapolis surrounded Manning with talented players. At running back, he first worked with Faulk. But when the Colts traded the star running back after the 1999 season, they replaced him by drafting exciting rookie Edgerrin James. At receiver, Manning had an incredible connection with the sure-handed Marvin Harrison, who had been a first-round pick in 1996. The tandem would eventually record more touchdown passes than any other quarterback/receiver combination in NFL history.

That was just one of many records Manning would break during his career. But his biggest task was more difficult. In the early 2000s, Manning and the Colts faced an uphill battle to get back to the Super Bowl.

Marvin Harrison's 1,102 career receptions, 14,580 yards, and 128 touchdowns were all Colts records when he left the team in 2008.

Tony Dungy is the all-time Colts leader in both regular-season and playoff wins.

CHAPTER 5

REACHING THE TOP

After consecutive playoff berths in 1999 and 2000, the Colts fell short in 2001. The team decided a change was needed. Head coach Jim Mora was let go, and the Colts brought in the soft-spoken defensive guru Tony Dungy. In his previous head-coaching job, Dungy had turned the Tampa Bay Buccaneers into a league power. Now he was arriving in Indianapolis to get the Colts over the hump.

It started well. The Colts won 10 games and returned to the playoffs. But the season ended a familiar way. On January 4, 2003, Peyton Manning walked off the field dejected. His Colts had just been thumped on the road in the playoffs by the New York Jets. In a 41–0 defeat, Manning had completed just 14 of his 31 passes for 137 yards and a pair of interceptions.

Despite early NFL success, Peyton Manning struggled in the playoffs in his first few seasons.

That was becoming a theme in his career. During the regular season, Manning smashed records and looked unstoppable. But in three playoff games, all losses, he had completed less than half his passes and thrown only one touchdown.

PLAYOFF WOES

While the Colts were excellent in the early 2000s, the AFC was loaded. The Pittsburgh Steelers were annual contenders, as were the Tennessee Titans. Meanwhile, the New England Patriots, led by quarterback Tom Brady, had won the Super Bowl after the 2001 season. In the 2003 playoffs, they appeared on the way to another.

That year, Manning and the Colts broke through with two playoff wins. Now they faced the Patriots in the AFC title game. The result wasn't close. Brady outdueled Manning, who threw four interceptions in a 24–14 loss. It wouldn't be the last time the two quarterbacks met in big games, though.

A year later, the Patriots beat the Colts in the season opener. Manning went on to throw a league-record 49 touchdown passes and lead the Colts to a 12–4 record. But in a divisional-round rematch, the Patriots spoiled the Colts' season again. In 2005, the Colts went 14–2, including a midseason 40–21 blowout of

Fans hold up a sign celebrating Manning's record-setting 49th touchdown pass in 2004.

Kelvin Hayden picks off a pass in the fourth quarter of Super Bowl XLI in February 2007.

quarterback Rex Grossman and dashed 56 yards for a touchdown to put a cap on the Colts' 29–17 win.

It wasn't a classic performance from Manning. Playing in heavy rain against one of the league's best defenses, he threw an interception and lost a fumble. But Manning also passed for 247 yards, including a 53-yard touchdown. The performance was enough to earn him Super Bowl MVP honors. Most importantly, though, it finally made Manning and the Colts the Super Bowl champions.

A LITTLE LUCK

Despite contending for several more years, the Colts couldn't add a second title with Manning. The closest they came was the 2009 season. The Colts went 14–2 and returned to the Super Bowl. There, they lost 31–17 to the New Orleans Saints. A late interception by Manning was returned for a touchdown to seal the loss.

HISTORY MAKER

When Indianapolis won Super Bowl XLI, Tony Dungy made history. He became the first Black head coach to lead a team to a Super Bowl championship. "I'm proud to be representing African American coaches," Dungy said of his achievement, "to be the first African American coach to win this. It means an awful lot to our country."

Dominant defensive ends Dwight Freeney, *left*, and Robert Mathis, *right*, combined for 230 1/2 sacks in their careers during the 2000s and 2010s.

After the 2010 season, Manning began experiencing pain in his neck. He had surgery in May, but when he found himself unable to throw a ball, he needed a second surgery to his spine that caused him to miss the season. Without him, the Colts stumbled to a 2–14 record, the worst in the league.

Manning waves to fans at his final home regular-season game in Indianapolis on January 2, 2011.

That left the Colts with the top draft pick for the first time since picking Manning in 1998. And once again, the draft featured a top quarterback prospect. This time, it was Stanford star Andrew Luck. Though Manning didn't want to leave the Colts, the team decided to start a new chapter by selecting Luck. "We all know that nothing lasts forever," Manning said. "Times change, circumstances change,

Andrew Luck set an NFL rookie record with 4,374 passing yards in 2011.

and that's the reality of playing in the NFL." The veteran quarterback went on to win another Super Bowl with the Denver Broncos. However, he's best remembered for his 13 seasons in Indianapolis. In announcing Manning's exit, team owner Jim Irsay made it clear that no Colts player would ever wear Manning's No. 18 jersey again.

"WE ALL KNOW THAT NOTHING LASTS FOREVER. TIMES CHANGE, CIRCUMSTANCES CHANGE, AND THAT'S THE REALITY OF PLAYING IN THE NFL."

—PEYTON MANNING

THE COMEBACK

With 13:39 left to go in the third quarter, Luck jogged onto the field. The Colts trailed the Kansas City Chiefs 38–10 in their wild-card playoff game after the 2013 season. In two seasons, Luck had proved himself to be a worthy successor to Manning. But now he needed to produce a miracle.

Luck dives across the goal line to score against the Chiefs in their January 2014 playoff game.

Within two minutes, Luck had led a touchdown drive. Four minutes later, he threw a touchdown pass to make the score 38–24. Though the Chiefs added a field goal, Luck kept charging. With 2:34 left in the third, he tossed a 12-yard touchdown strike to tight end Coby Fleener. Early in the fourth, Indianapolis running back Donald Brown fumbled on a run from inside the Chiefs' 3-yard line. The ball bounced back to Luck, who scooped it up and dived into the end zone.

Kansas City led 44–38 with 4:33 left when Luck fired a deep pass over the middle. The ball eluded two defenders and went into the hands of receiver T. Y. Hilton, who raced to the end zone for a score. The 45–44 victory marked the second-largest playoff comeback ever. And it showed that the Colts were ready to contend again.

BATTERED

The Colts' 2013 playoffs ended with a loss in the divisional round. But a year later, Luck took the Colts a step further. After a division title, the Colts reached the AFC Championship Game against the Patriots. Once there, however, they were roughed up by Tom Brady in a 45–7 New England win.

On top of being a gifted passer, Luck could also scramble in a way that the slow-footed Manning never could. However, Luck's running ability soon caught up with him. In 2015, he suffered a shoulder injury early in the season and a kidney injury later in the year. After the 2016 season, he had shoulder surgery that caused him to miss the entire 2017 season. Though he returned in 2018 and led the Colts to the playoffs, Luck shocked the football world by announcing his retirement just before the start of the 2019 season.

T. Y. Hilton, *top*, celebrates his game-winning score against the Chiefs.

COLTS TROPHY CASE

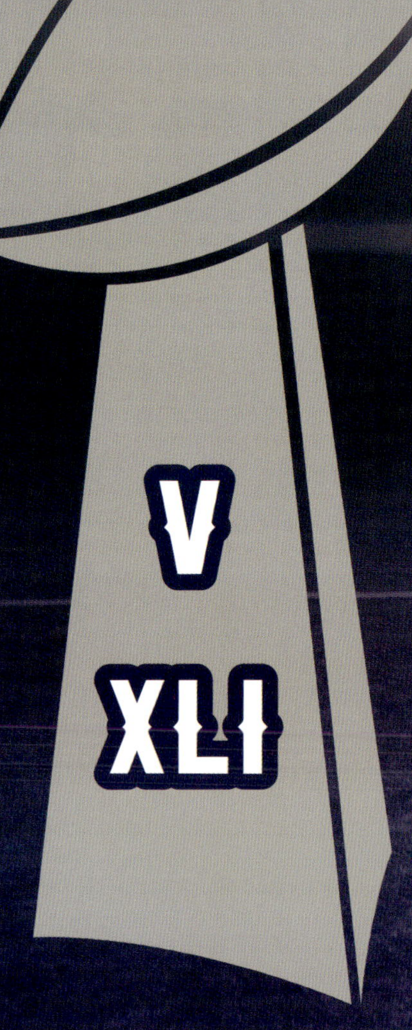

SUPER BOWL CHAMPIONSHIPS: 2

Super Bowl V – January 17, 1971
Super Bowl XLI – February 4, 2007

NFL CHAMPIONSHIPS: 2

1958, 1959

CONFERENCE CHAMPIONSHIPS: 4

1968, 1970, 2006, 2009

DIVISION TITLES: 19

AFL West: 1958, 1959, 1964
NFL Coastal: 1968
AFC East: 1970, 1975, 1976, 1977, 1987, 1999
AFC South: 2003, 2004, 2005, 2006, 2007, 2009, 2010, 2013, 2014

All stats are through the 2024 season.

Jonathan Taylor rushed for 1,811 yards and 18 touchdowns in 2021, both Colts records.

Citing his injuries, he said he was no longer having fun playing football.

The Colts returned to the playoffs in 2020 behind the stellar play of rookie running back Jonathan Taylor. However, another winning season in 2021 wasn't good enough to reach the postseason.

Though the Colts still had talent, they struggled to find a quarterback who could replace Luck. Fans hoped the team solved that problem when it picked Anthony Richardson fourth in the 2023 draft. With elite athleticism and a rocket for an arm, Richardson showed flashes of that potential before injuries cut his rookie season short. Then an up-and-down 2024 season left Indianapolis outside the playoffs for the fourth year in a row. However, his ups left fans hopeful that Richardson could still be the team's next great quarterback.

GLOSSARY

contender–a person or team that has a good chance at winning a championship.

contract–an agreement to play for a certain team.

coordinator–an assistant coach who is in charge of the offense, defense, or special teams.

draft–a system that allows teams to acquire new players coming into the league.

dynasty–a team that has an extended period of success, usually winning multiple championships in the process.

era–a period of time in history.

folded–went out of business.

franchise–an entire sports organization.

general manager–an executive who runs a team and is responsible for finding and signing players.

Hail Mary–a long pass that has a small chance of succeeding, usually made near the end of a game as a last-ditch effort to score.

merge–join with another to create something new, such as a company, a team, or a league.

overtime–an extra period of play when the score is tied after regulation.

pandemic–a widespread occurrence of an infectious disease.

rookie–a professional athlete in his or her first year of competition.

semiprofessional–something that pays, but not well enough to make a living.

shotgun—a formation in which the quarterback lines up 5 to 7 yards behind the center and takes the snap in the air.

strike—refusing to work as a form of protest, usually about things such as working conditions and wages.

turnover—loss of the ball to the other team through an interception or fumble.

union—a group that works together for a common cause.

upset—an unexpected victory by a supposedly weaker team or player.

veteran—someone who has played for many years.

wild-card—the first round of the playoffs.

ONLINE RESOURCES

To learn more about the Indianapolis Colts, please visit **abdobooklinks.com** or scan this QR code. These links are routinely monitored and updated to provide the most current information available.

INDEX

A
Addai, Joseph, 50
All-America Football Conference (AAFC), 13
Ameche, Alan, 14, 18, 19
American Football League (AFL), 26-27, 29, 31

B
Bailey, Aaron, 43
Baltimore Ravens, 43
Berry, Raymond, 14, 17, 18, 22-23
Brown, Donald, 56
Buckner, DeForest, 7

C
Chicago Bears, 16, 51-52
Cincinnati Bengals, 31
Cleveland Browns, 23, 25, 28, 31
Crockett, Zach, 42
Cuozzo, Gary, 25

D
Dallas Cowboys, 31-33
Dallas Texans, 14
Denver Broncos, 40, 55
Dickerson, Eric, 41
Dungy, Tony, 47, 53
Dutton, John, 39

E
Elway, John, 40
Ewbank, Weeb, 14, 21-22, 29

F
Faulk, Marshall, 41-42, 45
Fleener, Coby, 56

G
Green Bay Packers, 25-26, 27

H
Harbaugh, Jim, 41, 42
Harrison, Marvin, 45
Hayden, Kelvin, 51-52
Hilton, T. Y., 57
Hoosier Dome, 39

I
Infante, Lindy, 43
Irsay, Jim, 43, 44, 55
Irsay, Robert, 34, 38-40, 41, 43

J
Jackson, Marlin, 50
Jacksonville Jaguars, 5-6, 8-9
James, Edgerrin, 9, 45
Jones, Bert, 38

K
Kansas City Chiefs, 42, 56-57

L
Los Angeles Rams, 33-34
Lucas Oil Stadium, 9
Luck, Andrew, 54, 56-57, 59

M
Mack, Marlon, 7
Mackey, John, 23, 32, 33
Manning, Peyton, 44-45, 47-57
Marchetti, Gino, 14
Marchibroda, Ted, 37, 38-39, 41, 43
Matte, Tom, 25, 30
McCafferty, Don, 31
Memorial Stadium, 20, 39
Miami Dolphins, 30-31
Miami Seahawks, 13
Michaels, Lou, 26
Minnesota Vikings, 28
Mitchell, Lydell, 38, 39
Moore, Lenny, 14, 17, 20, 22
Mora, Jim, 45, 47
Morrall, Earl, 28, 29-30, 31
Mutscheller, Jim, 17
Myhra, Steve, 18

N
New England Patriots, 48-50, 57
New Orleans Saints, 53
New York Giants, 17-19, 20-21
New York Jets, 29-30, 47

O
Oakland Raiders, 31, 38
O'Brien, Jim, 32-33

P
Parker, Jim, 14
Pittman, Michael, 7
Pittsburgh Steelers, 14, 31, 37, 38, 42, 48, 50
Polian, Bill, 44

R
Reich, Frank, 7
Richardson, Anthony, 59
Richardson, Jerry, 20
Rivers, Philip, 9
Rosenbloom, Carroll, 14, 21-22, 31, 33-34, 39

S
Sample, Jerry, 20
San Diego Chargers, 37, 42, 44
San Francisco 49ers, 7
Shaw, George, 15-16
Shinnick, Don, 25
Shula, Don, 22, 23, 25, 28, 30, 31
Super Bowl, 27, 29-30, 31-33, 40, 42-43, 45, 50-52, 53, 55, 58
Szymanski, Dick, 14

T
Tampa Bay Buccaneers, 47
Taylor, Jonathan, 5-9, 59
Tennessee Titans, 48

U
Unitas, Johnny, 14-21, 23, 25, 27-28, 30, 31-32, 37, 40, 44

V
Vogel, Bob, 32